Raining U

RAINING UPWARDS
Henry Normal

Flapjack Press
flapjackpress.co.uk

Exploring the synergy between performance and the page

Published in 2017 by Flapjack Press
Salford, Gtr Manchester
flapjackpress.co.uk

ISBN 978-0-9955012-7-0

Cover art and flap illustration by Johnny Carroll-Pell
facebook.com/Art-By-Johnny-882499851852944

Printed by Imprint Digital
Upton Pyne, Exeter, Devon
imprintdigital.com

Dedicated to Sarah and Andrew Pell
for everything and more.

I would like to thank Linda Hallam, Paul Neads, Theresa Sowerby, Penny Shepherd and my wife Angela Pell for their help in bringing this collection together.

Contents

At the age of 22 I met Henry Normal in a flat in Crumpsall, a suburb of Manchester which at that time possessed about as much poetry as its name would suggest. Poetry was something in which I was well versed. I had just finished a degree in English and had studied it to death. Henry was the first living poet I had ever met. He introduced me to a netherworld where people showed up in rooms above pubs and read out loud as part of evenings that flirted with the new wave of stand up comedy, but held their own ground. Of course the borders of poetry are there to be flirted with, and on those nights they extended out towards rap in the hands of some and narrative comedy in the hands of others. The sheer panoply on offer made you question what poetry actually was. What qualifies an assembly of words to be classified as a 'poem'? What invisible line does a writer have to cross in order for bells to ring and the wreath of 'poet' be conferred? After three years of study I actually had little idea. Listening to Henry in a pub in Ashton-under-Lyne I started to realise. Here was a man with perhaps one less layer of skin around the heart, allowing him to feel what we all feel only quicker. A man who sees what everyone sees, but from two steps to the right and can then report his reconnaissance with a simplicity that makes you feel more intelligent. Someone in whose hands ordinary words find new atomic partners and spark previously unseen reactions. Here was a writer under whose touch the most mundane of places, people and consumer products were endowed with an unexpected dignity. Much of what I read at college has long since evaporated. There are fragments of Henry's poems that have remained with me since those days in north Manchester, butterflies that never quite left the room. This collection abounds with them. Honest, false-footing and proof that a 'poet' is someone who refuses to see themselves as a poet and rather exalts in the sheer extraordinariness of being normal.

"Do not be angry with the rain; it simply does not know how to fall upwards."
Vladimir Nabokov

Raining Upwards

The moon is leaving slowly

Every single star in the totality
pulls on my blood

Each individual atom
attracts

I am drifting
at the rate fingernails grow

If only
you could wrap your arms around me

Between neap and spring tides
as planets align
and the Earth slows

centrifugal force increasing
I am lifted

Emptiness
is an even number
neither positive nor negative

Created in the imagination
as beautiful
a perfect circle

A hole
into which all the numbers in the universe
divide

Hard now to believe
there was a time
before quantification of that
which doesn't exist

uncontained
impossible to communicate
Only an unnamed absence

Who wasn't out to sea didn't pray to God

There is enough water here to drown every soul on Earth

We sit and watch white lines
break upon black slate

Trees and shrubs I can't name
claw at slopes whose classifications I can't pronounce

The whole facia falls bent and crumpled
like a broken roller coaster rail

These veterans
a wall-planner of existence

Humanity huddles at the inlets

Though we don't say as much
we share a cathedral sky with the distant clouds

the abandoned buildings
the quiet fisherman

the Easter sun
and the loneliness at the end of the ocean

Why do we look for order and uniformity when

it is only though the unevenness
in the spread of hydrogen atoms
at the birth of the universe
that anything more exists

Through the patience of gravity on warps in space-time
through ultraviolet corrupting opaque clouds

through instability in generations of stars
through destruction and metamorphosis
on every scale

throuGh the random
and the chAos
the muTation and compliCation
the different
and the new

we arrive at that first connection within the womb
sparking
your
unique
brain
to life

The Second Punic War is not available on a tea towel

Fortifying lungs with calm
the first sight of snow for the
elephants from Carthage pulls
at the foothills of the Alps
now folded blue grey at dusk

Closing rays reach around peaks
clutch at clouds overcoming
mountains with long memories
one shadowing the other
ever into the distance

In the room of the hospice
we talk of anything else
Barbarians at the gates
Tectonic plates colliding
Invaders so far from home

The father of tactics sleeps
eventually humbled
bled by strategy unseen
We've learnt it is hard to change
direction within the charge

The toughest hide is fragile
I can but hope a plan will
form to delude my senses
as though one could charm cancer
as though Death himself would yield

As the ground accelerates towards you at an acute angle

If I tilt my head to the side
you are perpendicular
and the rest of this unholy mess
is at a slant

Italic trees in parallel
mark the degrees
ten past the hour

Dry leaves defy gravity
There is no slide to the east

Shadows brave the slope
The sun no longer certain
of its position

Toes grip for balance
Legs lengthen or shorten
to compensate

Fire-engine red you stand out
amid the muted woodland

You lean against the sky like Atlas
carrying all on your back

"And wilt thou bend a listening ear to praises low as ours"

After Henry Kirke White

Where shadows are deeper shoulders fall
you can allow time for the aged and infirm

The hut of the old people
is given over to young bodies bolstered by rubber

Two fold-out chairs culture clash
amid abandoned clothing strewn on rocks

A flow of blood for heart and brain
excuse enough to bring your own stick to the beach

Three legs confuse the sand
Shuffle and tap lost to surf

Easing down on the front
well ordered anarchy ensues

The ten yard line ebbs and flows, fits and starts
reacts and breaks at its strongest point

We are relatively static
as the sun reflects on the outgoing tide

The world washed and scrubbed
fresh for a new adventure

All that learning and all that love
how can this not be a better day

Walking away is made up of several moments

Wanting to walk away

Seeing the possibility of walking away

Deciding to walk away

Turning and walking

Realising you are walking away

Deciding to keep walking

Knowing you are not going to turn back

Realising you are no longer walking away

Realising you are just walking

Not being afraid to look back

Not being afraid to look forward

I am rendered immortal
my image digitally preserved
Ochre from the Ice Age
once immobile in this Sulawesi cave

The decay of uranium
confirms
over thirty thousand orbits
I have held my breath

From the right hemisphere of an early artist
I am born fully formed
This limestone you see behind me
this was our home

Now I will walk the world for him
Visit you
his descendants
in the place you call home

I have come to tell of a shared creativity
I have come to tell of an inner life
I have come to tell
he was not that different from you

A stream of consciousness meets the ocean

Like Rommel retreating from el Alamein
we are scattered across the sand

Waves clamber to reclaim the beach
leaving the man on his lounger as a pier

Another man patrols the shoreline
wearing a watch

The wind pelts my back with tiny meteors
acupuncture en masse

I take off my shoes
feel the grains on the flat of my feet

German dad in a mismatch of stripes
washes his kid's trunks in the swell

A cowgirl and Mrs Capone
model their new hats

There's a fat man in Speedos
like an egg in an egg cup

Striped awnings that offer a sliver of cover
contort in the breeze

as though invisible punkahwallahs
have gone apoplectic

Lovers enjoying their youthful bodies
trip themselves through the water

Teenage girls adjust bikinis
Yellow buoys bob like large bathtub toys

Mums slap suncream on infants' shoulders
like basting a roast

Ice lollies drip down sticks
Kids sit in holes the shape of cars and boats

Someone's asleep
with a towel over their head

A shanty town of windbreaks and umbrellas quiver
Futile mats instantly covered with sand

Young males show their prowess and agility
with two bats and a rubber ball

A small dog bounds from group to group
scaring the nervous

There's a disembodied head in the sea laughing
Abandoned dads build castles undeterred

A group of women stand at the water's edge
discussing sea temperature and the merits of immersion

The winner of the pinkest man of the year is revealed

A youth holds a rock the size of a skull
An impromptu Hamlet

then somewhere between shot-putt and discus
he hurls it into the sea

A boy carries a surfboard bigger than himself
A head, two feet and two hands float

A family re-enact the Olympic games
Long jump is easily mimicked

Surf boy tells his dad the story of his wave
his words crashing over each other

Too late a large woman in a thong bends down to stroke the dog
This could be any beach, any month, in any year

If it wasn't for a couple with a selfie stick
and the man with the e-cigarette

Nobody can remember who that is in the image

Is that me?
It doesn't look like me
I don't remember it being taken

It could be me
but what if I say it's me and it's not?
Am I living someone else's life?

Stealing someone's memories?
But then if it is me
who the hell am I?

I'm not this person am I?
I wasn't a moment ago
Now I'm this person and there's the proof

Have I been lying to myself all this time?
Do I have to make the decision?
Who am I to make that decision?

Fairy lights round a death bed

Tearing open the Christmas paper
it soon became apparent

Jutting out of the pillowslip
it had suggested itself at first glance

but disbelief had forced me
to re-appraise my suspicions

Now here it was confirmed
a ladder

Not a bright red ladder
Not a ladder adorned by Disney motifs

Just a plain ladder

The sort you might buy at any DIY store
I had not requested a ladder

The thought of receiving a ladder
had never crossed my mind

I had no more need for a ladder
than any other eleven year old

I checked to see if there'd been some mistake
but no, it was addressed to me

It was in my pillowcase
No-one claimed to know anything about it

There was no note or instructions
Ladders tend not to come with instructions

Altruism

We are slicing up Albert Einstein's brain
like so much corned beef
dissecting the universe
behind those sad eyes

The guillotine falls with razor precision
the slivers are wafer thin
there is a finite amount of tissue

If we could
we would take a scalpel to his mind

He will never know of our results

We may discover no more than with any other brain

We may discover we are not deserving

The remnants of a gymkhana

Closing my eyes in all this nature
seems a little churlish

It's the arse end of a farm
This ground is not designed for trainers

Man-made stuff sits scattered
like a junk yard

Candy-striped poles now caked in mud
lie like a kindergarten Waterloo

Traffic cones remain stubborn on sodden grass
Fallen leaves have outstayed their welcome

The rain dribs and drabs
like the last shakings of a drunk

The sky couldn't be more grey
Any British Standard colour chart would confirm

I can hear cars in the distance
Trains, helicopters even

In the field nothing moves
apart from the shimmering of poplars
forming a lofty chorus line

The gate is tinged green
like the wood is trying to re-root

This is not the rut I'm in
This is something different

Behind me a pale horse neighs
There's still hay to be had

Twigs and fences co-exist
Trees and timber
like life
living alongside the dead

The foetal position follows the curve of the lining
The placenta is circled to form a knot

The tongue is wrapped around the word 'mamma'
The sphere of the skull is soft

The child learns to judge the arc of the ball
The sun and moon mark day and night

A sail appears over the horizon
The outline of anatomy stimulates adrenalin

The foetal position follows the curve of the lining

An imaginary fly cannot be captured

After posh dessert in a paper dish
the debris of sugar scents the garden

This instant is an insect
Happiness the beat of a wing

A lazy summer evening recedes
at the pace of a picnic

Creation now sweetly attractive
our perception of time is a mismatch

Tea cups and beer glasses co-exist
as we share this flight of fancy

I appear to hold death in my hand
but mock gently as shadows stretch

You are intelligent and quick witted
Nothing will die today

in truth we both know
neither would harm the tiniest of souls

Though these human eyes are in need of focus
the joke we can see only too well

The shutter speed far too slow
timing is everything in comedy

Anticipation adds the necessary tension
It's there at your throat

Keep still, don't move
hold your breath

Anchor

There is something about a sense of scale
A small anchor is commonplace
almost a toy

But a real-size anchor
from a real-life ship
the sheer weight is impressive

Immovable
no tide or wind
can pull it away

Exhumed from the deep
it lies here
like a heart exposed

Sunglasses can make it seem darker than it actually is

We cast long shadows in the low sun
Though our shapes may be different
we are still connected

Outlines move across wet sand
and skirt rocks that reach for the surf
In this pause the elements are our playroom

We have made a companion of our solitude
I'm conscious of where my skin meets the air
how the pulse at the back of my neck softens

We turn our faces to the glow
recognise our temporary imprint
and resolve to make our way home

Pictures of you without me

When I see pictures of you
before we met
I see the lightness
the expectation
the optimism of a world unfolding
A world before

Then somewhere between a pantomime villain and cancer
I cast my shadow on your face
I know you are still there
and you would probably deny
anything but age and experience
pulling at your shoulders

but
when I see pictures of you
before we met
I wonder what pictures of you
would look like now
If we never had

An empty bottle for bashing
better than any toy
You are in control
there is no pretence at role play

This is nature unreserved
You lean forward
your brim upturned
not only the sun lights your face

This is a choice
not a compromise
This is authentic
not a substitute or a version

Expressing, playing, stimming
whatever name I give it
is only my invention
and won't alter the fun one bit

If the bottle was made of precious metal
it wouldn't necessarily be any better
The red dust complements the bright blue
of living water

You are no longer apart from the topography

Man in a glass booth

I have a speck of dirt on my window
Outside the Channel contorts and wrestles

Inside I am consumed by the tiniest of smudges
obscuring my view
pulling focus
snagging

It's probably bird shit

Seagulls and crows
don't even pretend to
mock innocence
as they flirt with the invisible

Raw nature
in all its certainty and vigour
prevails
unwitnessed

What I need is a little sponge on a stick
I think you can get them at the Pound Shop

then we'll see

The smell of freshly cut grass is a communication

Lying flat on my lawn
the core pulling me in
I wonder what message
the blades are releasing

This morning I have no argument
with wasps or bees
or the spiders who web
the pagoda

I half bury a stray fig
to give it a fighting chance
Even the weeds are safe
hanging on to the soil for dear life

The September sun
blesses my skin
its rays colliding with oxygen
bruising the sky blue

I try to feel the Earth spin
against the clock
Humans are not built to lie on grass
too many knobbly bits

My head needs support

Pain is telling me something

I'm already at my computer typing

This is already memory

I don't need to see his face to know it's him
the light has its own plans

In reality nothing is still as elements compete
A split second away there is another poem

If I want I can see a trail of silver
at the spill

or the ominous underbelly of distant concentrations
Everything I see is a reflection of this love

I can home in on the dislocation of arms
in motion

or glory in the contrast
of chemistry as liquid and gas

We may not see the same world at all
I hope yours is as full of splendour

"And can you, then, who have such possessions and so many of them, covet our poor tents?" - *Caratacus*

With a narrowing of vision
the mountains could be envious of the sea
All that fluidity

Envy is usually selective
One could say it's a form of greed
or wishful thinking at best

It's not that the mountains
would want to stop being mountains
or lose their height and grandeur

They would only want to add
that extra something
they admire in the nature of water

There would be longing of course
and a feeling of inferiority perhaps
A resentment within the core

How could the mountains compete
other than with molten rock?
It would not be the same

Hiding guilt in those eyes
that avoid the waves and tides
It would never be the same

And to think once these mountains stood
so proud
the sky itself was envious

And if you
should lose your heart to the sea
how then should the mountains feel?

I'd like you to know

When you feel you've handled the situation
When you've used the jargon
        applied the textbook
When you've selected only the supporting facts

        edited memory and redrawn history
When you've ignored the question
        and deftly changed the subject

When you've gone on the attack
        to avoid the obvious
        and leave no space for reply
When you think you've got away with it

When you're patting yourself on the back
        for being so clever
        I'd like you to know I can see your lies

You've got me but who's got you?

Even the Earth moves
vulnerable in space
like an egg in a pinball machine

Lights and sounds distract our attention
from the lack of substance
like seatbelts on a fairground ride
inadequate if the ride goes off track

We hold onto each other
and force a brave face
so as not to frighten the kids

Time, rust, friction, wear and tear
and the bolt sheers

The best you can do is hope
and try to save others
Let your body break their fall

Christmas at the end of the world

It seems all old Portuguese men dress the same
as though they've come to a conclusion

At the end of the world
there is a chair so big
those that sit on it become children

The weight of the ocean
undercuts the candy-striped rocks
Termites in silhouette iPhone the sunset

In this place that others have called sacred
a light and mirrors safeguard invisible ships
waves move sideways on the lumpy horizon

The Earth spins on your finger
delicious and small
the universe is infant once more

Too small to be a snowman
this could be a snowchild

I hold onto your hands
partly to warm them
but partly not

Two Brussel sprouts
a lemon for a nose
scarf and cap

We are not going to win any prizes
This is a family photo
of family
for family

It need be of no interest to anyone else
If you saw it in an album
you might well flick past without comment
a little embarrassed
that we would consider this worth presenting

Whether we are on a downhill slope
or uphill
is a matter of perspective

Our faces white as hoar frost
haunt these early learnings

When you were a baby
I put your name down for a school place
Paid a deposit

The money is no loss at all

I've always hated shiny apple selfish people
whose lives are one big wedding
where they are the centre of attention

Their opinions
their qualities
their relationship

We bring them presents
we take their photos
we laugh at their speeches

we dress up, we wait
we clap, we cheer
we eat their stupid cake

we go home
and we give it six months

I've been afraid
as long as I can remember

Not afraid of my brain becoming night
more afraid of failure

a particular failure
that of missing the point

I sometimes wonder if life actually exists
in the gaps between doing stuff

All the time spent waiting
and filling in

It would be ironic to arrive in Heaven
and find out

that
was the bit that mattered

then spend the rest of eternity
waiting and filling in

having
never quite mastered the art

The surface
of an alien brain

Tie-dyed green
and glassy grey

Little pools of imagination
cloudy and mysterious

Step carefully
with feet bare

Miniature Loch Ness monsters
crowd the crevices

loose stones lurk
in murky salt water

We bend to connect
and there is treasure

for certain
there is treasure

The sea encouraging
at a distance

like a parent
ready to rush in

Horizontal amid horticulture

As I lower my head to the grass
I am shorter than the chives

Self-seeded fennel towers over me
like a monument to liberty

A cornflower weaves the trellis to gain height
Life is in competition for sunlight

The beech trees aren't big enough yet
to warrant the term trees

The poppies have lost their flowers
but not their sense of purpose

New blossom stands alongside those that wane
Passion flowers drape like curtains beside the swing

I am no threat to anything that crawls or flies
I am at a level with the salvias though not as attractive

Olive trees dominate the skyline
The sapling of a silver birch stands like an exclamation

Figs ripen at their own pace
drawing yesterday's rainfall upwards

Ornamental thistles brave it out amongst tall grasses
too regal to be mistaken as weeds

Unseen birds whisper secrets in Morse code

Faint clouds scour the sky like someone
hasn't rubbed them out properly

Wild mushrooms hide in the undergrowth
like lost golf balls

Nearby hawthorn bushes catch litter
blown from the beach

I pick them tidy
and carry the distraction

A thin skin of fresh green
now protects the Downs

There's a field for mothers
and their newborn

a suspicion of rabbits
at pace

At the foot of the cliff
families watch their step

The tide is at its furthest reach
There is still a bite in the air

When the sun climbs
I am able to sit for longer

Though you are always more
than a name on a bench

touching the letters

is the nearest we can get
to an arm around the shoulder

I have shrunk with age and grief
I am not sure I have a soul left to steal

He has his mother's nose
a family resemblance in outline

Our weather-proof coats
sort of match
hooded against the torrent

Deepest blue obscures into black
on the inside
the lack of detail gives the impression
my head exists in space
like a hologram
or a dark snow globe

The mountain behind looks unreal
a photoshop composite
complete with derelict shelter

Only his hand on my shoulder
instils solidarity
and cohesion

The hailstorm has all but subsided
leaving us a little bruised
and buffeted

There will be better days
and worse
for certain

It's in the nature of ice
when the stone grows too heavy
it cannot be sustained in mid-air

I look to you
for confirmation
I am still alive

Hominin footprints in Laetoli

Covered with earth to preserve
volcanic ash suggests that which is absent

A black and blue marble
forms the palest of lanterns

All we touch in this world
bears our signature

From a warm little pond
to the chemistry of consciousness

from bowing on all fours
we have raised our heads to the heavens

Far beyond the constellation in Hollywood concrete
there are trace fossils on the Sea of Tranquility

As we teach each new child to stand
we move ever nearer the gods

Are other animals afraid of their own species?

Even on tip-toes the ceiling is too tall

From a distance though the halo we breathe
is nothing more than the shedding of outermost skin

Happiness is...
A trick
played on you by your body
to encourage behaviour
beneficial to its survival

I've lived in fear all my life
Fear of change
or the lack of it

There is fear...
and there is lack-of-fear
We could call this happiness

Anger is fear
Sadness is fear
Surprise and disgust
all fear

Jealousy is fear...
When I was young I was angry at God
for not loving me as much as he did others

and if sadly he didn't exist then
I was angry at the universe for not loving me
as much as it did others

Pinning this cloud to the page
it appears to take up less space

Happiness is perhaps
an illusion of control
or an acceptance
of the lack of it

I do a strange thing with
my head sometimes

I lift it up
raise my chin
look the world in the eye
defiant for no reason

This is who I am
this is what I am
deal with it

It's very unlike me

Deafness and social cohesion

I can't hear very well in restaurants
Let me clarify that

I can hear the background noise
just not the conversation
I'm supposed to be concentrating on

So people tell me jokes
and are disappointed by my lack of humour

Or proffer tough criticism
which I seem to take in my stride

Share secrets I never divulge

Ask me for things I never deliver
Questions I never answer

Make arrangements I never keep
Offer opinions I accept without argument

My wife has an eye for a photo
I am too conscious of duty
My father-in-law points the way
My son leans to be included
Only his grandma is camera ready
sunglasses on the top of her head
scarlet antlers marking the season
clashing with an array of pinks

I imagine a second image
like a spot-the-difference puzzle
where subtle changes are noted
My father-in-law facing forward
His wife not needing a seat
No bags under Angela's eyes
My hair without grey
Ear defenders no longer evident

There's more to lemons than being yellow

Alone with my lad and the waves
we brave the collapse of the cliff edge
A wading fisherman is bullied by the tides

There is a mist way out at sea
but the freshness on the margin
invigorates the skin

Debris around our feet
Life trying to keep hold
Lungs expand to fill all thought

I am here and consciously alive

We've crossed the line between
existence and exaltation
as though commonplace

Whether a shrine or a mirage
the shoreline is never long enough

Unmarked

A grave without a headstone
is just a scratch of ground

Overgrown
littered with autumn leaves

Easily mistaken for a short cut
Even the grave digger is embarrassed

Without tender husbandry

A gap in a row of teeth

Only recognised by the name
on the neighbouring plot

Somehow so different from ashes
scattered in a chosen setting

The absence lies within others

Naked before God
bare bones

left wanting

If you never saw this tree it must be difficult to imagine its glory

There is an absence of tone to my muscles
A lack of colour in my hair

We are in the Algarve off-season
across from where my wife buys gluten free

There is an absence of tree, unnoticed
Neither of us is native to this land

Unused chimneys on empty houses
are unconcerned

Even the surrounding grass is without life
the steps to the car park untrodden

Lines marking out unoccupied spaces
are unaffected

There is no wind to play with the palm leaves
now only imagined

There is nothing here to lean upon
On another day it stood taller than me by far

Now scissored cuts criss-cross the stump
there are no rings to confirm age

A lack of shade
filling the space of what once was

Soaking

Even in this late sun
it's a wonder my feet don't grow
They are sodden

There's a leak somewhere around the nozzle
and I wrangle the hose
as gallons flood back finding a level

I like that watering forces me
to look at each plant
individually

My new drinking partners
sunbaked khaki
nurtured back to lush green

Glorying in technology
I adjust the spray to a fine rope
to reach the stragglers at the fence

A kink strangles the flow
and I smooth the loops
to restore the charge

I have a special attachment for the lawn
The twirl throws globules around like
a dog emerging from the sea

a dervish dance
the whiplash spitting
like a liquid spirograph

life restored
at the turn of a tap
Just a circular movement of the fingers

The self-deception of priority

I board the bus to the flight alongside the wheelchairs
and the families with small children
Mothers holding babies displace
elderly dads on the end seats

There's one arrogant-looking lone man
in his fifties who was first in the queue
and there's me

He looks the type that is used to getting
preferential treatment
and I worry I have that appearance
or indeed the attitude itself

I appreciate the irony as we stand and wait
for non-priority boarders to make up the numbers
before the bus heads off to the plane steps

Flying on my own always makes me self-conscious
I am redefined, no longer an elderly dad
already standing to leave seats free for families

The arrogant-man leans back against the glass
and I see the outline of his out-of-shape stomach
against his tucked-in Polo shirt

My Polo shirt is un-tucked to avoid such unsightliness

My wife tends to book priority boarding
as a habit to head-off problems with our autistic son

Here now I look indulgent
like a businessman sneaked onto a flight
last minute by an overworked secretary

It would take too long
to explain to each and every passenger
and in the grand scheme of worries
I'm sure mine are not priority

The spiral staircase casts a shadow

Maybe there's a certain age
when you no longer fear skin cancer
where the sun is slight
its rays are gratefully gathered in

A choice of vivid colour
widens the pupil
awake and vital
youth cramming the dial

The contrast of light and shade
like a before and after diagram
Yourself dark upon your work
or content without trace

The March of Progress

With respect to Rupert Salinger and Richard Dawkins

Evolution is only a straight line looking back
There is no one destination

Without guarantees
we step into the unknown
in all directions

From the age of reptiles
to the age of mammals

The selfish gene is not immortal
Fidelity is seldom total on
this entangled bank

This is what is
not what ought to be

We stumble, we fall, we fail
and we learn

Under gravity
we adapt to seasons and tides
through chance as much as design

We illustrate from this juncture
only what has survived

But in the richness of human culture
we carry the lives of those that falter

As again
we step into the unknown
in all directions

At the hearth of the winter sky

I put my faith in the automatic handbrake
and walk down the slope

You can take photos now directly at the sun
and although detail is obscure
silhouettes are epic against the falling star

We walk until there is only rock and waves
Looking back across the terrain
the scale is enhanced

Later waiting for a hot chocolate competes
against the final glory of refracted light

Sanctity in coral and ash

I try to catch the eye of the waiter
to register annoyance
but relent

Travelling in 4D

When my dad died
I was given his watch

Strange, as we never
spent that much time together
absent within the same room

Our days were marked by
coins stacked on the mantelpiece
electric, gas, bread and milk

I won't leave the watch to my son
he has no need to measure hours
Days are marked with meals and sleep

outside time or in perfect sync
A zone uncharted in any atlas

We are in the world as wide as it is
side by side

He chooses to walk with me
I choose to walk with him

With Johnny's arm around my shoulder
the spin of the Earth slows

Slitting my own throat

When I was a young man
I tried to shave all the beard from my face

Not just the hair I could see
but the hair I could feel

I scraped away again and again to remove any trace
any suggestion of shadow pending

What came was a huge rash
matted blood and rough skin

until I learnt
to cut the hair you can see

and be content that more
was to come

Auditioning for the X-men in the Wetlands

Drawn back to the lagoon
two shaved apes

neither of which speak the language
doing nothing much
not a thunderbolt in sight

This day wouldn't fill a postcard
The landscape lounges

We are happy mutants
sixty percent water
three percent orange juice

The sea and sky
an agreed grey

Elephant clouds
stepping the Pillars of Hercules
Pale amber kissing the dunes

The smile on my son's face
making the moment immortal

Without trespass

Your hands are together
as though in prayer

The image before you
has his arms raised
as though wanting to be picked up

Without trespass
I try not to project my hopes
and accept all possibility

Your hands might be caught mid clap
The image might be exalting the sky
You are more than my perception

You may be warming your hands
against the weather
The image may well be waving

You could be rubbing chalk between your palms
The image could simply be trying to surrender

I sit with my dead brother
by the Atlantic
Two superheroes
disguised as my wife and offspring
try out their new costumes in the splash

I wrap myself in my son's coat
the zip a Rubik's cube

We know the routine
fresh orange, side plate and olives
hold down the paper place mats
from the magpie wind

The tide edges into the river
reversing the flow

This moment is my life
My life is this moment

Soon it will be dark
everything I now see will still be
only with the absence of light

If I close my eyes
you are still here

Orphan

There is a plant in a pot separate from the garden

A cordyline with green and purple leaves
like a baby palm tree

It does not share the earth with the orange trees
or the spongy grass

Its soil now surrounded by terracotta
may well have originated from the bed nearby

but here roots are confined
nature contained

This individual adorns the patio no further
from the rest of life than you might scatter seed

Pilgrimage for the agnostic

It is reverence that marks the moment
To make time and space
religious or not
reflection brings you closer

In the want of a better place
I come to find something tangible beyond myself
though I know
this is not where you are
and is never where you were

Only your body is buried
in this formal row

You live within me

You have always lived within me
even before
Why then
would death change that

It is I myself
who have brought you here
and it is with me
you will leave

Our love is ahead of us
He walks the length of the beach without once looking back
Islets puncture excited turquoise
Jets scar the sky
comets with neutered tails

We are at the point where the earth moves
The vertical lines of rock
look like burnt toast on a rack
or black plates in a dishwasher

A breeze blows my hood at the back of my neck
With a trick of perspective
I hold the future in the palm of my hand

My boy hears music that I can't
he covers his ears

I am reflected in your eye

Trying to explain Jesus
to my son I realise
there is what I believe
and what I want to believe

These walls feel as old as hope
and my heart aches for a miracle
or the allowance
of the possibility of a miracle
somewhere
under the possibility
of Heaven

I wipe my eyes embarrassed as
my wife returns from the gift shop
leaflet in hand

The donkey we saw in the masonry
is a bull
to signify St Luke

The angels on the ceiling
slaves stolen by the infante

I give the guide to a young English man entering

I'm not aware if he has a son

This is the likeness of things that no longer exist

Those clouds you see
have long since passed

The horse has long since become glue
or dog food

Each leaf has been shed
each blade of grass grown out

This hair you see has long since
been swept from a barber's floor

The clothes either gone to charity
or the tip

Each cell of skin
has been replaced several times

Even the shadows on the soil
would no longer be cast the same

The sheet music of Microwave Background Radiation

Of course, the Big Bang was silent
as sound can't travel through a vacuum

In the afterglow
molecules formed
and vibrations rippled energy waves
light years in length

A cosmic chord
the scream of an infant birth
building into a deep rasping roar
and ending in a deafening hiss

Like a jet engine descending into tv static
The first tree falling in the forest unheard

The echo of this heavenly choir
deep below the octaves of the human ear
become bacterium on a bowling ball

At its smallest everything is sound
a universal string section
the DNA of reality

If you listen you can hear harmony
in the pulse of your blood

and the sadness of minor chords
heard by the first humans

Sand suspended in mid-air
defies the natural order

Johnny presses his teeth
against the back of his hand
to contain the excitement

My wife stands ready
as I bash the bottom of the
sun lounger once more

We can only see the effect
captured by a single frame

I'm unsure what delight
my son is experiencing

We can only see the effect
captured by a single frame

Eskimo kiss

One hand supports soft scalp
another removes all obstacles
you are safe again
surrounded by family

There is warmth in this welcome
gravity embraced
eyes lock and focus as never before
Generations whisper greeting

Biology reveals new sensations
a world immediate and infinite
Face to face with creation
you breath the same air

Tiny fingers realise a first grip
am I part of you?
are you part of me?
there are no extremities today

Skin touching skin
a most human hello
essential learning
you are connected still

The foghorn has long since given up

Despite sea fret
Vitamin D warms my eyelids

The immediate is sharp
but distance bleeds into haze
like I'm inside an abandoned snow globe

Sitting on the terrace in my shorts
my bleach-white legs
stare out the UV rays

If you join the dots
on my limbs
a picture of psoriasis forms

Another gift passed down
from father to son

There's a fox that likes
to mark out his territory
in my garden
always on walls or steps
never on grass

If I put my knees together
and spread my feet apart
the rays can work
directly on the infection

My back will have to wait its turn
My black tea has now
ceased support

There's a green tinge
to the bones of trees

A hot shower this morning
has left my pores open
to all comers

A fly is drawn to the paraffin
on my head
I am expecting to spontaneously
combust at any time

A helicopter
rails against
the bird kingdom

Two tall chimneys
interrupt my view
They are for show only
but not from this angle

The February breeze
still has bite
Everything competes
to force my hand

I've other duties
and responsibilities
on the clock

If I half turn
I can see my phone screen clearer
in squat shadow

This may be the last of the sun
for a while
If I write a poem
I can hold on a little longer

What would I have done better?

My head is on upside down
Iron filings on opposite poles of a magnet

I can feel but I can't think
and even then it's confusing

Without imagination
monkey bars are just bars

Pyjamas, it appears, can be worn any time of day
Everything money can't buy I don't understand

I'm searching for clues in old memories
as if the answer was there all along

The world outside my brain is too big
in every direction

I could stare at yesterday forever
and still not understand

What would I have done better?
Everything

The movement of shadows on the moon

Nowadays I find loading and unloading
the dishwasher a form of meditation

All news is weather
and I still wait for my real life to begin

Iridescent
It's the colour you don't see that's being absorbed

A different man stands before the ocean
skin as white as face cream

Only now this little bit of carbon
has finally forgiven God

I've learnt that the breastbone of an angel
needs to be far larger than mine

That once you're in the ground
you can't own your own grave

That blind mole-rats rub tears
over their body for defence

I am a man without a telescope
numbering the stars

My language is scraps
fallen from the grown-up's table

My regrets come so fast
they leave vapour trails

There's nothing I own
but these smudges of cloud

I have slept too long in one position

I've learnt Heaven doesn't solve
the need for meaning

it just shifts the location

Against caution
you choose to be generous

Whether through habit or will
you seem at ease with giving

as though kindness was natural
as though empathy inbuilt

And while reality crowds our eyes
and frustration and greed stalk unfettered

you choose to open your arms
against all rationale

as though to convert the world
one at a time

I am besotted

First prize

As you climb the podium
we applaud
there is no grand speech

We are the only witnesses
if you discount
the shrubs and the sky of course

This is for fun
but motivation is there
balance and co-ordination

You are the hero
you have overcome
you are ready to play

There are no medals big enough
no metals shiny enough
to do you justice

Two wooden boxes
on a piece of grass
make you taller

But
you are already taller
you are already taller

You won't find a box to tick on any form for this

It must have taken some time to build that wall
and there are so many walls
and there've been so many lives spent building them

We sit together
our backs to the stones
each in our own breath

No-one can see what catches our eyes
only a quiet body language
You could be any teenager

I could be any dad
neither revealing superpowers of
good or evil

Your hand hovers
unconcerned with personal space
We are not afraid to touch in passing

We have arrived at an understanding
almost unnoticed
we are on the same side of the wall

This is merely blossom, fruit will follow

Palm trees know how to bend to a hurricane
and regain their shape

Unsteady
I spot-check my senses

My body creaks like these old sun loungers
The breeze is in danger of blowing my tan clean off

No matter how they itch
you should never scratch spots

You can scrape your nail around them
to ease the temptation and fool your nerve endings

Only on the final day of a holiday
am I about to relax

On a mountain of lemon trees
I sit on a bench at the bottom of the garden

and look back to where I live
like staring at myself from inside a mirror

The sun behind my shoulder
spoons like a lover

Leakage

I have one photo of you crying
a sole tear preserved in black and white
your cheek as yet soft canvas
sunlight surrounding your understanding

There appears a question
in the window of your eye
your pupil undilated
a confusion perhaps leaking out

This interaction is in close up
the background lacking focus
your pale lips unmoved
unable to control the tide

In the fifteen years since
you have not shed saltwater
on the outside
although

occasionally I catch the same look
on that same child face
only fleeting
as though unsure of the flood

There is a ghost on the shoreline taking a selfie

You are probably the only person
in that whole ocean
swimming with their 17 year old son

The shape of the earth is shifting
Dry sand whisks around my feet

Diagonal lines in the cliff
show how once the land was at a different angle
before the world buckled and bent

There's a hazy cloud but with no edge
like a hollow fog

Thin trees on the slope lean south
A natural groyne lies like a brontosaurus on the beach

Black rocks skulk beneath the surf
volcanic sharks with unforgiving teeth

We are a line of shells at high tide
One ship is on the horizon
big enough to carry us all

Fresh air cocoons my brain
My eyes feel haunted

We eat olives and cheese before the main meal arrives

Fish heads stare at me from the side plate
They know I've put them at the corner of the table to distract the flies

The ship nears and veers away from the setting sun
a small boat in its wake

I am disguised as an old man trying to dress too young
I kiss the scars on my son's arms
and wonder what you see

As though infinity could be turned off

I watch as a small ball floats
blown by the breeze

It tours the ripples
and seems to come to rest
at the shallow steps

Then around again the current stirs and carries
this vulnerable toy
revolving green and blue
in and out of shade

The water's skin contorts
causing reflections to shiver
The wind plays peek-a-boo
A gust blurring the surface
like frosted glass

At the edge of the infinity pool
droplets fall away
pulling on the strongest of bonds
atoms cascading after atoms
That weakest of powers, gravity
drawing everything closer

In my car at speed
I remember seeing water
climb the windscreen
as I accelerated
into rain
A temporary victory
almost as though I could outrun the universe

The difference between falling down and having a fall

I can no longer kid myself
that I've not peaked

My dad in the shaving mirror
can see through me

It's about mitigating the rate of decline
Matching an acceptance level

from the way up but without
the hope of better to come

I've fallen down many times
and picked myself up saying

"That's one less slip
that will catch me unaware

A useful education
A positive experience"

Then
there's having a fall
and seeing that long slope
stretching out before you

Whether a series of small but inevitable slips
        or one big fat fall from grace

                with each step
                I move ever nearer to

                the bruise that will never mend

Sofa at the centre of the constellation

You are easy with contact
body language like slang

Crimson girders
form a backbone

Worn leather
cushions the light

Cosmology and domesticity
seem strange bedfellows
but everywhere is local when you're there

We have put a hole in the ceiling
to let in the night

Heads tilted to the dark
we find ourselves in others

On one side a detailed history
cites the shades of the spectrum

We have travelled all the way to the moon
to discover the Earth

The walking wounded at Lidl

My psoriasis does not qualify
for priority parking

My wife eases her dodgy back
out of the vehicle

As eyes view us with suspicion
a blue badge authorises the windscreen

My father-in-law reveals nothing
of his need for statins

Only my mother-in-law looks the part
leaning heavily on her stick

A stroke and heart attack at the same time
qualifies her for a shorter walk to the supermarket

Earlier I saw her lift the weight from the world
Immersed in water

her limbs as free as summer
no time limitation in sight

Once inside the shop we are in public
A world of plenty is laid out before us

Fridges hum, tills bleep
muzak underscores decisions made

A little girl with no physical ailments
squeals constantly for attention
She too has her story

My son wears his ear defenders
as the two of us sit back in the car
out of the way
and wait

in the disability space

Vibrations

Electricity in the trees
Cicadas call to life

With some over a decade
in the dark
it's no wonder
they sing so loud

Dragging a needle
across vinyl
their song of courtship
can deafen the human ear

Seeking security in numbers
their only tactic
for immortality
is to overwhelm

When next
nymphs shed their skin
and brave the light
will I still have voice?

Earth reclaims the threshold

The door to the old house
has been retired to the garden
The pergola forming a frame
softened by variegated ivy

Unbolted, the oak wood opens
into an hidden corner where
a child's trampoline lies weathered
beneath neighbouring branches

Bamboo walls surround the nets
already going native
The dark beneath the springs
has become a cellar

There are new shoots amid rust
shrubs snuggling up
climbers reaching out
to lock elbows

Though I sense the spirit
of the law of nature
I don't have the language
to do justice to this fragrant anarchy

Still the door I recognise
functional and rectangular
crafted and domestic
not as yet buckled by the elements

The intoxication of tidal shift

From the outside a whirlpool
looks an impossibility

like the mapping of milk in coffee
but there is beauty in this energy

The simple draining of a bath
or the passing of an airplane

can curl the elements. My son
brings out the best in people

I see the curl in them
as he enters the room

as if he gives each permission
to be themselves

Before moving into the heart of a new lawn

If you look closely some strands of grass
are far longer than others

The darkness of my jeans absorbs the light
heating my thighs like a radiator

I have a windmill that turns in two different directions
like the minute and second hands on a clock at odds

This is a bench in my garden
I've never sat on before

Halfway down the brick steps
like raked theatre seating

Green in many shades is becoming overgrown
Honeysuckle entangles a metal sculpture

Birdsong loops and rises
Clouds on high lay dissipated like flour through a sieve

I have memories in this space from early fatherhood
climbing frames, splash slides, inflatable pools

ponds of frogspawn and water lilies covered with wire
all now landscaped out of mind

Landed

Once in my shorts I'm officially on holiday

Fishing stray palm leaves
with the pool net is therapy

almost an ancient mystic art
requiring meditation and oneness
with chlorinated water

the resistance to the pole at depth
loops and curls the current

sleeping snakes stir
contort and evade
to no avail

There is a satisfaction in returning
each leaf to the garden with a little jolt
the ghost hood inside out

Also a satisfaction
in the pure blue of the pool
without distraction

balance restored
for a moment

A small corner of the world as it should be

The shaded garden

Some of these plants could be weeds
Some are exotic

The bamboo I recognise
It has outgrown me and then some

The Japanese acer stands delicate in the corner
its leaves like ornamental copper

Assorted trees and hedges on the south border
have become one, imitating jungle

the track of the lawn mower the only sign of civilisation
Kamikaze wasps patrol

Slugs have left little leaf on one poor plant
the remains – a dying stencil

A lighter acer edges the pergola
looking like an oriental side dish

There is a small wooden hut
almost an hidden temple

Climbers hang across the doorway so
you have to bow as you enter

Kissing the top of my own head

Everyone says I look like my uncle John
only not yet as old

He once told me
of the worst day in his life
and it was the same as mine

I kiss the top of my son's head

I'm not sure where we are
but those are my lips
and that's Johnny's blond hair
and that's all that's needed

I remember my uncle John
kissed the urn as he
scattered my brother's ashes

After that
how could I not
hug this man

There are layers of cloud moving in different directions

As the wave retreats
it catches the pebbles
like the keys of a musical box

This scree on the foreshore
becomes like a cheese grater for water
The sound almost a small round of applause

Each wet stone blinks a glint of sun
before the next surge
towards my abandoned clothes

A short walk west
there is a pregnant woman in the sea
possibly eight months swollen

Her partner and two toddlers
at her side
on an invisible cord

At this distance
they could be any nationality
speak any language

Light rolls on each undulation

In the background
a row of headlands
line up to bless the ocean

This is a photo of me not smiling

I have been taught
not to smile

I haven't been taught
what to do instead

So what we have
is an absence of smile

This is a photo of me
not smiling

This is a photo of my body
not smiling

This is a photo of the outside
of my body
not smiling

I've no recall
of what is happening inside
and no photo to help me

A little slope of meadow outside my window

It's only mid-May but the snowball tree
is past its best

The dragonflies have left and
only the wood pigeons and a few friends
insist on being noticed

The magnolia is already saving itself
for next spring
The wind has blighted the upper leaves

With cherry blossom now long gone
the main tree stretches out for sunlight
and makes the most of its shaggy haircut

In between the red bricks of the car port
small scraps of green blotch like
felt tip on graph paper

at the bottom of the bank the grass is thicker
a scouting party of daisies appear diffident
There's a sole dandelion feigning innocence

A squat dwarf willow crouches like a country hat
My wife wants to put two cartoon eyes on it
to make it a muppet

At a discreet distance a thin tree with paler leaf
is propped by a wooden post
a few branches don't have any foliage at all

This latest addition appears healthy but almost
like life is drawing straws

Altamura Neanderthal

An old European cousin entombed
biology now chemistry
more cave than man

Amid stalactites
and stony globules
as though bejewelled

hollow red eyes seem to plead
for lids to bring back the darkness

Experts fear rescue lest he fractures
Lazarus in limestone

He has no descendants to mourn him
you can hurt him no more
let him sleep
let him dream

Through this likeness
I validate my claim

I identify with the ancient
the unimpeachable authority

My human features mock
the spectre

More than a face
I am healed-blank

Transformed
invulnerable

All controls suspended
God-like

with deliberate intent
I am emergent

Naked as I am
beneath
I am no longer afraid

I've never had an email worth keeping forever

I have a letter rack
with no letters in it

It used to hold bills
but never a letter

Why I've acquired it
and why I keep it at all
these are both mysteries

If I get a letter
or several letters
I do have somewhere to put them

So I entertain at least
the possibility
of getting a letter

a letter worth keeping

Reclaimed

My camera can't capture the breadth
of this wind-teased ocean
or the authority of volcanic mounds
that fall away far beyond the beach

180 degrees of untamed depth
180 degrees of fire made solid

Johnny pinches his mum's skin
playful in this physical domain

Small barnacles polka dot
black boulders on the beach
smoothed by abrasion

All this ground upon which I stand
is just a bigger rock rising out of the sea

I am anchored in the present by family
We whoop and shout into the high wide sky

For a full 360 degrees our world
remains beautifully autistic

Pivot

Looking back at my new home

the grass slope tilts the bench
a little like a dentist's chair

The solar panel on the reclaimed slates
resembles a minimalist painting

There is more in the air
than you might first imagine

The baseline from the road
dulls as it bends over and round the trees

In my son's window the backs of nutcrackers
parade as triangle, the tallest in the centre

I can see my usual seat on the terrace
now high above my head like a thought bubble

I am avoiding responsibility
hoping to justify my absence

by filling the moment with
the pause untaken

the sky is blueberry ice cream

Self-portrait of the poet as an old man

I point my spots accusingly
at the sun

As I drink water
my corrugated fingertips smooth

I feel it won't be long
before I leave this precious flesh

I can't remember the numerous times
I had sex in my youth

but I remember the times
I was certain I felt love

I could be obscure here
as a means of protection

but the truth of this communication
is

I am now the age my brother was
when he died

It occurs to me
the greatest tribute
I can pay him
is to live the kind of life
I wanted him to have

A victory of sorts
Each day a battle hard won

For him
I wanted so much

Near miss

North towards the Bay of Biscay and home
I am in stasis

At high altitude
the view down from the plane
is like looking through a microscope

An alien underworld
of random lines and patches of colour

An eggshell tapped with the back of a spoon
Algae forming in furrows
Lakes like spilt ink

Scrapes of snow
where perhaps a giant has pulled his boots
across the summit

until, in peripheral vision
the coast surprises
littered with dust from broken tiles
A straight line drawn with the wrong hand

Then
arcing over the water
a wagon train of clouds head west

White flecks in the deep blue confuse
An inversion of space

Lifting my head in reflex
for an instant I see other lives
pass in the opposite direction

Despite our relative speeds
almost in slow motion
other eyes catch mine

Considering all that exists in three dimensions
and the amount of time in any one life
and given the ability to alter speed, height and direction
you would hope
collisions would never occur accidentally

I look around for reassurance
teenagers submitting to screens
parents policing infants
all oblivious to the closeness of the inevitable certainty

The cabin staff retain their fixed smiles
There's a curtain across the front of the aisle
that's not fooling anyone
like a dishcloth trying to cover a windshield

and I wonder if each pilot saw
the surprise on the other's face

later
as we land
all my problems
become my problems
again

Hold me with certainty in this heavenly chaos

Lead me by the hand
to where pirates sleep

where air has crossed the sea
to find me

where my skin shines
and my lungs draw deep

and leave all fear and doubt
behind me

Late renewal

Speeding on the way to the cemetery
I'm thinking about overtaking a hearse

I console myself in that
there's a set time period in which to receive a ticket

And I wasn't going to write any more poems about death
although I do love the words 'bone garden'

Even today
I can't bring myself to take out gravestone insurance
It smacks of a lack of faith

I park in the marked area
outside the gates

and hope no-one breaks in
whilst my mind is elsewhere, off guard

Removing old flowers and dusting the stone
gives me an excuse to stroke the grave
run my fingers along the words
and numbers that go back a lifetime

I break open the plant food
that makes the new flowers last longer
though I know
no-one will be there to see them

No-one but the deceased that is
and that's who they were for anyway

Witness

This is a tree that knows me
I played under its branches as a child

Its weathered trunk may well be heavier
but these longer limbs can still embrace

Its shadow has stretched in the late afternoon

Though all around has been relabelled progress
it has set itself in this fickle landscape and
reached an accommodation with the sky

Of course, the sun is the same sun
but it has no sense of loyalty

There is commitment with a tree

This is an old friend
that knew well
those we've lost

When I'm gone
it will still know

and it will remember
that I spoke of you

Moon in the morning sky

Like a dinner guest
still there at breakfast

Its appearance is the same
only the context has changed

easily mistaken for a small cloud
but for the expanse of clear blue

Reflected light marks
half its full shape

To complete the picture
requires imagination

or a memory of what was once revealed
or at least basic understanding of geometry and cosmology

It sits in the west
in no hurry to slip away

I am the only living thing in my garden
not facing the sun

The blanket of green surrounding me
varies in detail at closer inspection

Deep reds and burnt orange
fight for attention

Tiny blue-purple buds emerge
as though a little shy

Olive green is easily distinguished
Bushes and shrubs soon stand out

like when concentrating on the hard bits
of a jigsaw puzzle

Each leaf is a child's drawing
Shapes and sizes now too obvious to have been missed

Small birds insist it's morning
A digital alarm that won't be muted

The wind strokes my hair

The moon has definitely moved
in relation to the yardstick of the tall cactus

Now lower in the sky
it nears the tops of the terracotta roofs

It seems only by looking away
distracted for a moment
can I perceive movement

I feel a warmth at the back of my neck
as I watch the slowest of goodbyes